Who Was Martin Luther King, Jr.?

Martin Luther King, Jr.

D0030163

Who Was Martin Luther King, Jr.?

by Bonnie Bader

illustrated by Elizabeth Wolf

Penguin Workshop

For Sophie and Tony—EW

PENGUIN WORKSHOP
An Imprint of Penguin Random House LLC, New York

If you purchased this book without a cover, you should be aware that this book is stolen property. It was reported as "unsold and destroyed" to the publisher, and neither the author nor the publisher has received any payment for this "stripped book."

Penguin supports copyright. Copyright fuels creativity, encourages diverse voices, promotes free speech, and creates a vibrant culture. Thank you for buying an authorized edition of this book and for complying with copyright laws by not reproducing, scanning, or distributing any part of it in any form without permission. You are supporting writers and allowing Penguin to continue to publish books for every reader.

The publisher does not have any control over and does not assume any responsibility for author or third-party websites or their content.

Text copyright © 2008 by Bonnie Bader. Illustrations copyright © 2008 by Elizabeth Wolf. Cover illustration copyright © 2008 by Penguin Random House LLC. All rights reserved. Published by Penguin Workshop, an imprint of Penguin Random House LLC, New York. PENGUIN and PENGUIN WORKSHOP are trademarks of Penguin Books Ltd. WHO HQ & Design is a registered trademark of Penguin Random House LLC. Printed in the USA.

Visit us online at www.penguinrandomhouse.com.

Library of Congress Control Number: 2007023064

ISBN 9780448447230   50 49 48 47 46 45 44 43 42

Contents

Who Was
Martin Luther King, Jr.?

Growing up in the South was not easy for Martin Luther King, Jr. He was born in 1929, when black people were treated very differently than white people. One day, Martin's father took his young son to buy a pair of shoes. The store was empty. But the white shopkeeper told them that they would have to wait in the back of the store.

Martin's father got very angry. Why did they have to sit in the back of the store? If he couldn't buy shoes for his son in the front of the store, he would not buy them at all. He took Martin by the hand and led him out of the store. As they walked down the street, his father said, "I don't care how long I have to live with this system, I will never accept it."

The "system" in the South kept black people apart from white people. It was called segregation. Black children and white children went to separate schools. Black people had to ride at the back of the bus. As he grew up, Martin decided to fight for change. But it was a peaceful fight.

Martin led marches. He banded people together in protests. He made speeches. Many people listened to his words and joined his nonviolent fight. Martin Luther King, Jr., fought using his words, not his fists.

Martin Luther King, Jr., had a dream—a

dream that all people could live together in peace
and be treated equally. And though he died over
forty years ago, his dream lives on.

Chapter 1
A Perfect Boy

On January 15, 1929, a baby boy was born in the city of Atlanta, Georgia. The doctors said he was perfect. His parents were so happy. They named him Michael, the same name that his father had. But when little Michael was five, his father decided to change both of their names

to Martin. So now, the little boy became Martin Luther King, Jr.

Young Martin had a very happy home life. He had an older sister named Willie Christine. (Everyone called her Chris.) He also had a younger brother named Alfred Daniel. The Kings lived in a large house on Auburn Avenue in Atlanta. Their neighborhood was comfortable. No one was very poor or very rich.

There was a lot of love in Martin's family.

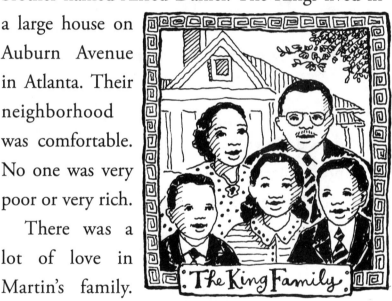

The King Family

Martin never remembered his parents arguing. Martin's mother, Alberta Williams King, was very soft-spoken and easygoing. Her father was a well-known minister. After high school, she went to college, which was something that not many black women did back then. Alberta had a warm personality, and Martin always found it very easy to talk to her.

Martin's father, Martin, Sr., was a large man in many ways. He weighed about 220 pounds and was filled with self-confidence. Martin, Jr., admired his father very much. His father's family was very poor and lived in a rundown shack. They were sharecroppers. A sharecropper is a farmer who does not own his own land. Instead, he works on another farmer's land and gets some of the crops for himself. Martin's father worked hard to get his high-school and college diplomas. After college, he became a minister of the Ebenezer Baptist Church in Atlanta.

Ebenezer Baptist Church

The Ebenezer Baptist Church was like a second home to Martin. He sang in the church choir.

He went to Sunday school and made many friends. It was there that Martin learned to get along with all kinds of people—kids as well as teachers.

One of Martin's good friends was white. The boys had known each other since they were three years old. The boy didn't live near Martin, but his father owned a store across the street from the King home. Martin and the boy were always together. But when they turned six, they started school. Martin went to a school for black children. The boy went to a school for white children. One day the boy's father told his son that he could no longer play with Martin. Martin ran home and cried to his mother. It was the end of the friendship.

That night at dinner, the family had a long talk. This was the first time that Martin realized how many white people felt about black people. Even so, his parents told Martin not to hate white people. It was his duty as a Christian to love everyone.

Martin's mother told him that he should always keep a sense of "somebodyness"—that he was important—even though the outside world was telling him he was not.

As Martin Luther King, Jr., grew up, he became more and more aware of the problems facing black people, especially in the South. Everywhere he looked there were "Whites Only" signs. Blacks could not go into many hotels, restaurants, and stores. Blacks could not even drink out of the same water fountains as whites. In many cities, blacks had to ride in the back of a bus. If they tried to sit in the front, they were thrown in jail. And if black people wanted to go to a movie theater, they had to sit way up in the balcony. These rules were called Jim Crow laws. And they made Martin very angry.

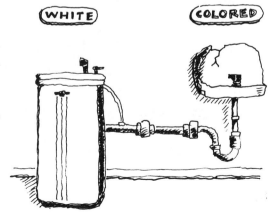

JIM CROW LAWS

THE TERM "JIM CROW" WAS STARTED AROUND 1830 BY A MINSTREL PERFORMER. MINSTREL PERFORMERS WERE ENTERTAINERS WHO TRAVELED AROUND THE NORTH AND SOUTH PUTTING ON SHOWS. THEY WERE MOST POPULAR BEFORE AND AFTER THE U.S. CIVIL WAR.

IN ONE SHOW, A WHITE SINGER BLACKENED HIS FACE WITH CHARCOAL TO LOOK LIKE A BLACK PERSON. HE DANCED AROUND IN A SILLY WAY THAT MADE FUN OF BLACK PEOPLE. HE SANG A SONG THAT ENDED WITH THE WORDS "I JUMP JIM CROW."

SOME PEOPLE THINK THAT THIS CHARACTER WAS BASED ON AN OLD BLACK SLAVE OWNED BY A "MR. CROW." BY THE 1850S, THE JIM CROW CHARACTER SHOWED UP IN MANY MINSTREL SHOWS.

BY THE TIME OF THE CIVIL WAR, THE TERM "JIM CROW" WAS A NEGATIVE WAY OF TALKING ABOUT BLACK PEOPLE. AND BY THE END OF THE 1800S, RACIST LAWS WERE CALLED JIM CROW LAWS.

In high school, Martin had to take a long bus ride to and from school. He always walked to the back, where the other black people sat.

Once, Martin and a teacher traveled by bus to Dublin, Georgia, for a speech contest. Martin won the contest and was very proud. On the way home to Atlanta, the bus driver ordered Martin and his teacher to give up their seats to white passengers. When they did not move right away, the bus driver became angry. It was the law, after all. They ended  up standing in the aisle for the ninety-mile ride. But Martin told himself, "One of these days, I'm going to put my body up there where my mind is." He knew that one day he would have a seat up front.

Chapter 2
School Days

Martin Luther King, Jr., was always a very good student. He loved to read and make speeches. He studied very hard and skipped two grades. At just fifteen years old, he graduated from high school.

That summer, Martin worked in Simsbury, Connecticut. It was Martin's first time in the North. He had a job in the tobacco fields. He was surprised to see how different life was for blacks in the North. Black and white children went to the same schools. There were no separate restaurants.

Martin dreamed that this could happen in the South, too. If only there was some way he could make this dream come true.

Martin returned to Atlanta to attend Morehouse College. This was the same college that his father had attended. All the students at the school were black. All the teachers were black, too.

At first, Martin wasn't sure what he wanted to study. He knew that he wanted to spend his life

Morehouse College

helping black people. But what was the best way to do that? Perhaps he would follow in his father's footsteps and become a minister. Or maybe he would become a lawyer.

In college, Martin Luther King, Jr., read an essay by a man named Henry David Thoreau. The essay was written in 1849. In this essay, Thoreau said that people have the right to disobey unjust laws. In Thoreau's time, the United States still allowed slavery. Thoreau wanted to protest slavery. He felt the government was wrong to allow it. So he refused to pay his taxes. As a result, he was thrown in jail. But Thoreau did not mind being in jail. He was making a point. Martin liked the way Thoreau thought. He also liked that Thoreau protested in a peaceful way.

Two of Martin's favorite college teachers were ministers. Because of them, he decided to become a minister as well. As a minister, Martin could speak out against segregation. He could show his people how much he cared.

When Martin Luther King, Jr., was only seventeen, he gave a sermon at his father's church. He wasn't a minister yet, but the sermon was heartfelt and inspiring. His words not only touched the members of the congregation, but his father as well. The very next year, Martin became a minister and also an assistant in his father's church.

In 1948, Martin graduated from college. He was nineteen. Martin's father wanted him to stay at the Ebenezer Baptist Church. But Martin wanted to continue his education. In September, he entered Crozer Theological Seminary, a school of religion, in Chester, Pennsylvania. Out of one hundred students at the school, only six were black.

At Crozer, Martin studied the teachings of people such as Mahatma Gandhi, the first leader of modern-day India. Like Thoreau, Mahatma Gandhi believed change could come from peaceful protests.

In 1951, Martin graduated from Crozer. He was the top student in his class. But he still thought there was more to learn about helping people through protest. So he moved to Massachusetts, to study at the Boston University School of Theology.

In Boston, Martin met Coretta Scott. Coretta had grown up in Alabama, but she was in Boston studying to be a singer. On their first date, Martin drove his green Chevrolet to pick her up. Over lunch, they talked about how hard it was to be black in the United States. They also talked about how people could live together in peace. Martin was impressed by Coretta.

MAHATMA GANDHI

· Gandhi ·

MAHATMA GANDHI WAS A POLITICAL AND
SPIRITUAL LEADER OF INDIA. HE WAS BORN ON
OCTOBER 2, 1869, IN THE CITY OF PORBANDAR.
AT THE AGE OF EIGHTEEN, GANDHI WENT
TO LONDON TO STUDY TO BECOME A LAWYER.

AFTER COLLEGE, GANDHI WENT TO WORK
IN SOUTH AFRICA WHERE BLACK AFRICANS
WERE TREATED AS SECOND-CLASS CITIZENS.
GANDHI SOON FOUND OUT THAT INDIANS WERE
TREATED THE SAME WAY. HE WAS ASKED TO
TAKE OFF HIS TURBAN IN THE COURTROOM. HE
HAD TO RIDE IN A SEPARATE CAR ON TRAINS.
THESE EXPERIENCES MADE GANDHI DECIDE
TO LEAD PEACEFUL PROTESTS. HE BELIEVED
THIS WAS THE BEST WAY TO SHOW THAT
DISCRIMINATION WAS VERY WRONG.

LATER, BACK IN INDIA, GANDHI PLAYED
A GREAT PART IN FREEING HIS HOMELAND
FROM BRITISH RULE. EVEN THOUGH HE SPENT
MANY YEARS IN PRISON, GANDHI PRACTICED
NONVIOLENCE THROUGHOUT HIS LIFE.

SADLY, GANDHI DIED VIOLENTLY. HE WAS
KILLED ON JANUARY 30, 1948, BY NATHURAM
GODSE, WHO WAS A HINDU RADICAL. HE
THOUGHT THAT GANDHI WAS RESPONSIBLE
FOR WEAKENING INDIA. TODAY, GANDHI'S
BOOKS AND TEACHINGS LIVE ON AND HAVE
INSPIRED MANY PEOPLE, INCLUDING MARTIN
LUTHER KING, JR.

After only an hour, Martin knew that he and Coretta were going to get married one day. And he was right! On June 18, 1953, they were married at the Scotts' home in Marion, Alabama.

The young couple lived in Boston. Martin had to finish his studies at Boston University, and Coretta had to complete her work to become a music teacher. When he was done with school, he became Dr. Martin Luther King, Jr. Martin was now ready to start his life's work—but exactly how would he do that?

Chapter 3
Martin Gets a Job

Two churches, one in Massachusetts and one in New York, wanted Martin to become their minister. While Martin was deciding which job to take, another letter came—from the Dexter Avenue Baptist Church in Montgomery, Alabama. The church, which had no minister, invited Martin to come down and preach.

On a clear winter day in January 1954, Martin set out to visit the church in Alabama. On the drive he listened to one of

his favorite operas on the radio. The music and the beautiful countryside made the four-hour drive pass quickly.

During the drive, Martin practiced the sermon he was going to deliver the next day in Montgomery. By the time he got there, he was nervous. He was not afraid to speak in front of people. At his father's church, Martin stood up before crowds and preached. But Martin knew that if his sermon tomorrow was good, the job as minister would be his.

Martin wasn't sure he wanted to live in the South. He knew that life in the North was easier for blacks. And fairer. Still, the church in Montgomery sounded like a wonderful place, and he wanted to make a good impression. Should he show the people that he was smart? Should he tell them all about his education? No. Martin knew that all he had to do was the same thing he had done before in churches: speak from his heart and help people pray.

MONTGOMERY, ALABAMA:
THE CRADLE OF THE CONFEDERACY

ON JANUARY 11, 1861, ALABAMA VOTED
TO "SECEDE FROM THE UNION." THAT MEANT
SEPARATING FROM THE REST OF THE UNITED
STATES. IN A SHORT TIME, TEN OTHER SOUTHERN
STATES VOTED TO SECEDE AS WELL. ONE REASON
THE STATES DIDN'T WANT TO REMAIN A PART OF
THE UNITED STATES WAS THAT MANY PEOPLE IN
NORTHERN STATES WANTED TO END SLAVERY.

ON FEBRUARY 18, 1861, IN MONTGOMERY,
JEFFERSON DAVIS WAS SWORN IN AS THE

PRESIDENT OF THE
CONFEDERATE STATES
OF AMERICA. THE FIRST
CONFEDERATE FLAG
WAS FLOWN FROM A
BUILDING THAT IS NOW
THE STATE CAPITOL.

THIS IS WHY MONTGOMERY
BECAME KNOWN AS THE CRADLE OF THE
CONFEDERACY.

IN APRIL 1865, THE NORTH WON THE CIVIL
WAR, WHICH PUT AN END TO SLAVERY AND
THE CONFEDERACY.

Sure enough, Martin's sermon was so good that the people at the Dexter Avenue Church asked him to become their pastor.

Martin talked with Coretta. She, too, shared Martin's fears. Could she find a good job in the South? In the North there were more opportunities for black women. Martin and Coretta also talked about what it would be like raising children in the South.

In the end, Martin and Coretta decided to live in Alabama. After all, the South was their home. And, more importantly, at the Dexter Avenue Church Martin could help fix some of the problems of local black people.

BROWN V. THE BOARD OF EDUCATION

AROUND THE SAME TIME THAT THE KINGS DECIDED TO MOVE TO ALABAMA, A VERY IMPORTANT CASE CAME BEFORE THE SUPREME COURT. IN TOPEKA, KANSAS, A BLACK THIRD-GRADER NAMED LINDA BROWN HAD TO WALK A MILE EVERY DAY TO GET TO SCHOOL. LINDA'S FATHER TRIED TO ENROLL HER IN A SCHOOL THAT WAS CLOSER TO HOME, BUT THE PRINCIPAL REFUSED. THE SCHOOL WAS FOR WHITE CHILDREN ONLY.

THIS CASE, AND OTHER CASES LIKE IT, CAME BEFORE THE NINE JUDGES OF THE SUPREME COURT. ON MAY 17, 1954, ALL NINE JUDGES OF THE COURT AGREED THAT "SEPARATE" SCHOOLS BY DEFINITION COULD NOT BE "EQUAL." WITH THAT REASONING, THE IDEA OF "SEPARATE BUT EQUAL" WAS STRUCK DOWN. ALL PUBLIC SCHOOLS HAD TO ACCEPT BLACK AND WHITE CHILDREN.

Chapter 4
Riding the Bus

Martin started his job as the pastor of the Dexter Avenue Baptist Church on September 1, 1954. In his sermons, he persuaded church members to register to vote. Voting was one way to change unjust laws. He also encouraged them to join the NAACP—the National Association for the Advancement of Colored People. The NAACP is one of the oldest civil rights groups in the United States. It was formed on February 12, 1909. Its purpose is to help minorities get equal and fair treatment when they look for a job, buy a home, or apply to a school. These are just a few examples of civil rights.

After living in Montgomery for about a year, Coretta gave birth to a little girl—Yolanda Denise.

Coretta, Yolanda, and Martin

Martin called her Yoki for short. Now the Kings were a family.

Only two weeks after Yolanda was born, something happened that changed U.S. history. On December 1, 1955, a forty-two-year-old black woman named Rosa Parks got on a bus in Montgomery. Instead of going to the back of the bus, she sat down in a seat at the front. The bus driver told her to move. But Rosa Parks refused, and she was arrested.

ROSA PARKS

Rosa Parks

ROSA PARKS WAS BORN IN TUSKEGEE, ALABAMA, ON FEBRUARY 4, 1913. AFTER ROSA'S PARENTS SEPARATED, SHE AND HER MOTHER MOVED TO THE FARM WHERE ROSA'S GRANDPARENTS LIVED. ROSA WAS HOMESCHOOLED UNTIL SHE WAS ELEVEN. SHE BEGAN HIGH SCHOOL, BUT SHE HAD TO DROP OUT TO TAKE CARE OF HER SICK GRANDMOTHER. IT WASN'T UNTIL AFTER SHE WAS MARRIED THAT SHE FINISHED HIGH SCHOOL.

BY 1943, ROSA HAD BECOME ACTIVE IN THE CIVIL RIGHTS MOVEMENT. SHE JOINED HER LOCAL NAACP CHAPTER AND THE VOTERS' LEAGUE.

ROSA WORKED AS A SEAMSTRESS AT A DEPARTMENT STORE. SHE RODE THE PUBLIC BUS TO AND FROM WORK. AFTER HER ARREST

ON DECEMBER 1, 1955, SHE SPENT THE NIGHT IN JAIL. SOME PEOPLE SAID THAT ROSA DID NOT GIVE UP HER SEAT BECAUSE SHE WAS TIRED. ROSA SAID THAT THEY WERE RIGHT—SHE WAS TIRED OF GIVING IN!

ALMOST ONE HUNDRED YEARS EARLIER, THE CIVIL WAR HAD ENDED AND SLAVERY WAS ABOLISHED. BLACK PEOPLE WERE NO LONGER SLAVES, BUT IN MANY PLACES REAL CHANGE DID NOT COME UNTIL THE 1950S AND 1960S, WHEN MORE BLACK PEOPLE BEGAN DEMANDING THEIR RIGHTS. MANY PEOPLE THINK THAT ROSA PARKS'S PROTEST—THAT ONE LITTLE ACT—WAS THE START OF THE MODERN CIVIL RIGHTS MOVEMENT.

Black leaders, including Martin Luther King, Jr., met to discuss Rosa Parks's arrest. Martin and the others came up with a plan. They would not ride the city buses to school or to work. This kind of protest is called a boycott. If the blacks of Montgomery stopped riding the buses, then the bus company would lose money. Perhaps then the government would change the laws.

Monday, December 5, 1955, was the day the boycott began. Since Monday was the start of a new school and workweek, people would have to take cabs or find rides in cars. Some would even have to walk. But Martin believed the boycott would send a strong message. If black people couldn't sit wherever they wanted, they would refuse to take the buses.

On Monday morning, Coretta and Martin woke up early. They peeked out the window to look outside at the bus stop. A bus pulled up. It was empty! Martin jumped into his car and drove

around the city. Almost all the black people he saw were riding in cars or walking. Later he learned some had to walk more than ten miles to get to where they were going!

The first day of the boycott was a tremendous success. But it needed to continue. People would have to give up riding the buses the next day, and the next day after that. They had to continue the boycott until the law changed.

White leaders in the Montgomery city government were angry. The city buses were losing money. But, still, the leaders did not want to change the laws. Instead, they tried making things harder for black people. The police commissioner told the taxi companies to charge higher fares so that it would be too expensive for most people to take taxis. They would have no choice but to walk.

But Martin and the other black leaders had a plan. They helped organize car pools. Many people—both black and white—volunteered to drive people taking part in the boycott. It was a good example of peaceful protest. Peaceful protest, however, also could be dangerous.

Martin was arrested by the local police. They said he was speeding in his car. Martin knew that he was not. The police wanted to scare him into stopping the bus boycott. Then a firebomb was

thrown onto the porch of his house. Martin was frightened for his family. But that did not stop him.

The boycott lasted over a year. Finally, the Supreme Court of the United States said that laws separating whites and blacks on the Montgomery buses had to end.

Martin was overjoyed. Now it was time for people to ride the buses again—sitting wherever they wanted to sit! Early in the morning on

December 21, 1956, three other leaders of the boycott came to Martin's house.

Reporters followed the men as they walked to the nearest bus stop. The reporters shouted out questions. Cameras flashed in Martin's face. This was a momentous day. When the bus arrived, Martin and the other leaders got on. The reporters followed. Martin took a seat right up front. On his face was a great big smile.

Chapter 5
A Peaceful Fight

Integrating the buses in Montgomery had worked. But Martin Luther King, Jr., knew that this was just the beginning. Martin and other black leaders met in Atlanta, Georgia. They formed a civil rights group called the Southern Christian Leadership Conference—the SCLC. On February 14, 1957, Martin became the head of the group.

In the South, civil rights leaders faced growing violence. One man's home was bombed. So were several churches. Then a service station and a cab stand were bombed. Martin urged everyone to remain calm. "We must not return violence under any condition," he said. He knew that his advice was hard to follow.

Martin's speeches made him famous in Montgomery. Wherever he went, thousands of people showed up to hear him. People even ran up to him on the street to ask for his autograph.

On May 17, 1957, Martin spoke at a gathering called the Prayer Pilgrimage in Washington, D.C. The march took place on the third anniversary of the passage of *Brown v. The Board of Education.* On the day of the march, thousands of black and white people gathered in front of the Lincoln Memorial. The speakers asked the government to pass a civil rights bill. This bill would guarantee all people in the United States equal rights under the law.

An important part of the civil rights bill would be to make sure every adult citizen was allowed to vote. At the Prayer Pilgrimage, Martin said that was the most urgent request to President Dwight Eisenhower.

While Martin was marching and speaking, Coretta was busy running the King household. On October 23, their second child, Martin Luther King III, was born. Martin said of Coretta, "I am indebted to my wife, Coretta, without whose love, sacrifices, and loyalty neither life nor work  would bring fulfillment." By this time, Coretta wanted to become much more involved in the movement. Martin, however, preferred that she stay at home raising their children.

THE FIFTEENTH AMENDMENT

IN 1870, THE FIFTEENTH AMENDMENT OF THE UNITED STATES CONSTITUTION GAVE MALE U.S. CITIZENS WHO WERE TWENTY-ONE OR OLDER THE RIGHT TO VOTE. (WOMEN—BOTH WHITE AND BLACK—DID NOT GET THE RIGHT TO VOTE UNTIL 1920.) BUT ALL OVER THE SOUTH, BLACK PEOPLE WERE STILL KEPT FROM VOTING. THEY WERE TOLD THAT THEY HAD TO PAY A "POLL TAX" BEFORE THEY COULD VOTE. MANY WERE TOO POOR TO PAY.

SOME BLACKS HAD TO TAKE TESTS TO PROVE THAT THEY COULD READ AND WRITE. IF THEY COULDN'T, THEY WERE TURNED AWAY. THEY COULD NOT VOTE FOR PRESIDENT. THEY COULD NOT VOTE FOR CONGRESS. THEY COULD NOT VOTE FOR LOCAL LEADERS. NOT ONLY WAS THIS UNFAIR, IT WAS AGAINST THE LAW.

In 1959, Martin did agree to take Coretta along on a trip to India. Martin wanted to see the land where his hero Gandhi had lived.

As he traveled through the country he saw that India was divided between the very poor and the very rich. Many people did not have jobs. Many slept out on the streets. Rich people, on the other hand, had beautiful homes and fancy clothes. Yet even with so much poverty, there was peace among the people. Yes, they were poor, but they did not take their troubles out on anyone.

Martin visited some of the places that were special to Gandhi. He and his group went to a place called Bambi. It was there that Gandhi had started a walk of more than two hundred miles to protest a tax on salt. Gandhi's walk began with eight people. The number grew to thousands. Some say that more than a million people ultimately joined the walk. Gandhi told his people, "If you are hit, don't hit back; even if they shoot at you, don't shoot back. Just keep moving."

Martin had a wonderful experience in India. When he returned home, he was even more convinced of the power of peaceful protest.

In 1959, the King family moved from Montgomery to Atlanta. It was hard to leave Montgomery, but Martin wanted more time for civil rights work. He could not be a full-time minister. He told his congregation, "History has thrust something on me which I cannot turn away." In Atlanta, Martin Luther King, Jr., would become the co-pastor of the Ebenezer Baptist Church, his father's church.

By the year 1960, the civil rights movement was spreading throughout the South. Black students and white students staged "sit-ins" at lunch counters. Students would sit together at a "whites only" lunch counter and wait to be served. Often,

the police would drag them out. But the students never fought back when arrested. Sometimes people yelled and spit at the students. Some threw rocks at them. No matter how many students were put in jail, the next day others would go "sit in" at the same lunch counters. They kept on because the fight was something they believed in.

Martin took part in the sit-ins. On October 19, 1960, he was arrested at a lunch counter in a department store in Atlanta. Over two hundred students were arrested that same day. They were all taken to the Fulton County jail. Martin told the judge that the sit-ins pointed out racial injustice. He wanted to make people in Atlanta see how wrong it was to have whites-only eating places. He said, "I must honestly say that we firmly believe that segregation is evil."

Five days passed, and Martin and the students were still in jail. Black people in Atlanta were very worried. Finally, the store owners dropped the charges, and everyone was set free. But many white people were still angry with Martin. They wanted him back in jail.

On May 4, 1960, the police stopped Martin in his car. They gave him a ticket for driving in Georgia with an Alabama driver's license. Martin thought, at worst, he would just pay the fine in court.

Instead, Martin was taken away, his legs put in chains, and driven to a state prison more than two hundred miles away. The ride to the prison was long. Martin was hungry. He was thirsty. He was scared.

When his followers learned what had happened to Martin, they tried their best to get him out of prison. They made calls to Vice President Richard Nixon and Senator John F. Kennedy, who

were running against each other for president.

Richard Nixon

At first, neither man wanted to help. They were afraid of angering the white voters. When reporters asked Nixon about Martin Luther King, Jr., being in jail, Nixon said, "No comment."

Finally, one of Kennedy's friends convinced the senator to help. First, Kennedy called Martin's wife, Coretta. She was pregnant with their third child, and she was very upset. John F. Kennedy told Coretta that he and his brother Robert

John F. Kennedy

Kennedy, who was a lawyer, would do everything in their power to help Martin.

Robert Kennedy called the judge who had sent Martin to jail. He wanted to know why Martin couldn't post bail. (Bail is money paid to the court that allows someone to remain free until the trial.) Now the judge agreed to set bail. Martin was freed.

Kennedy campaign workers printed millions of leaflets that said Nixon's "no comment" remark showed that he was a man without a heart. Martin's father, Martin Luther King, Sr., decided to vote for Kennedy now.

John F. Kennedy won the election that November. He was the first Roman Catholic president. Catholics in the United States had faced prejudice, too. That was one of the reasons many black people voted for JFK. Perhaps his own experience as a Catholic would make him more understanding of the problems of race in America.

Chapter 6
Freedom Riders

By 1961, there were not as many "whites only" lunch counters left in the South. But far too many waiting rooms, bathrooms, and restaurants in bus and train stations still had separate areas for blacks and whites. It didn't matter that the courts said this was illegal. Martin Luther King, Jr., spoke to President Kennedy, but the president did not take quick action to fix the situation.

On May 4, 1961, a group of students boarded two buses in Washington, D.C. They were traveling to the South. At some of the rest stops, the black students sat in the "whites only" waiting rooms. Again, they were staging peaceful protests. In Anniston, Alabama, the tires of one of the buses were shot out. A bomb was thrown in the window of the other bus. As the frightened riders ran out of the bus, they were attacked. The trip was over.

But the students did not give up. More groups rode buses from the North to the South. Again, students were attacked. Many were put in jail. These brave young people became known as "freedom riders."

One night, a group of freedom riders held a meeting in a church in Montgomery, Alabama,

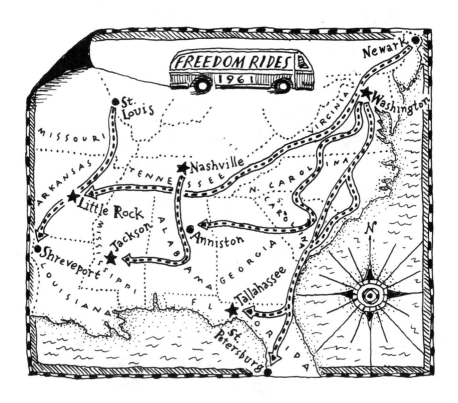

where Martin came to speak. A crowd outside threw stones and bottles at the church. But Martin urged everyone inside to stay strong. Together, they sang the freedom song "We Shall Overcome." Finally, the angry crowd left.

Was this the end of segregation in these places? No. The bus station in Albany, Georgia, for example, refused to give up a whites-only waiting room. So a man named Dr. W. G. Anderson started a group called the Albany Movement. This group staged sit-ins and boycotts. For months, Martin led marches all over Albany.

Once again, Martin was put in jail. Martin wanted to serve his sentence of forty-five days. After only a couple of days, however, Martin was freed. He had been kicked off buses and out of stores, and now he was being kicked out of jail! Yet after all the marches, and more time in jail, Martin and the rest of the leaders of the Albany Movement were faced with defeat. The segregation laws in Albany remained—at least for the time being. While some people might have given up, Martin looked at the setback as a beginning. His fight would continue.

Chapter 7
Freedom Comes to Birmingham

Martin Luther King, Jr., understood that the civil rights movement would suffer defeats. But now he was more determined than ever to prove the power of peaceful protest. He looked for the city with the toughest Jim Crow laws. It was Birmingham, Alabama. If Albany, Georgia, was bad, Birmingham was worse. Schools were still segregated in Birmingham. The water fountains were marked "colored" or "white."

Birmingham's police commissioner was Bull Connor. He was very

Bull Connor

tough on black people. He made them afraid to speak out against Jim Crow laws. Even the white people who did not like segregation were afraid to say anything.

Martin and the leaders of the Southern Christian Leadership Conference had a plan. Besides sit-ins at lunch counters, meetings were held at black churches all around Birmingham. At churches, protesters talked to people. They talked about peaceful protest. They sang freedom songs: "We shall overcome, Black and white together, We shall overcome someday." As Martin knew, the songs inspired a crowd; they gave black people courage for a good cause.

The Birmingham protests began. After three days of sit-ins, thirty-five people had been arrested. Now it was time for the second part of Martin's plan.

Martin and the leaders of the SCLC decided to boycott white businesses. Martin knew this would anger store owners. Almost half the people living in Birmingham were black. Without black customers, stores would have a hard time making money.

On April 6, Martin organized a march to the Birmingham City Hall. Many people joined this march. Bull Connor was growing angry. He and the policemen took clubs and beat some of the

protesters. Police dogs were let loose. But the people did not run away. Instead, they became stronger.

After ten days, five hundred people had been sent to jail. Some were released on bail, but about three hundred remained locked up.

Up until this time, Martin had not taken part in the marches. If he joined in, then he'd be arrested. And if he was in jail, he wouldn't be able to stay in charge.

On April 12, Martin and the other leaders of the protest met in Martin's hotel room. Martin's father and brother were there, too. Martin Luther King, Sr., wanted his son to come home. Easter was on Sunday, and he wanted Martin back at church to preach. Some of the other leaders thought Martin should stay and lead a protest. Other leaders did not want him to march because they feared he would be arrested. And still others thought that Martin should try to raise money to bail out protesters from jail.

An argument started. Martin left the room to think and pray. When he returned, he was wearing jeans. (He wore jeans whenever he went to jail.) Martin had made up his mind: He would join the protestors on their next march.

Just as expected, Martin was arrested. Usually, he was able to call Coretta right away. But this time, he was not allowed to make a call. After two days, Coretta, who had recently given birth to their fourth child, became frantic.

Martin had been put in a jail cell all by himself. No one was allowed to visit, not even his lawyers. The cell was small and very dark. The only light came from a tiny window near the ceiling. Martin was scared. He worried about his wife and family. He worried about other protesters.

Even white ministers were against Martin. In a letter to the *Birmingham News*, eight white pastors said that protest was wrong. They felt the SCLC should not break laws. They said that Martin and his group were stirring up hatred and violence.

In response, Martin wrote a long letter. Since he did not have any paper in jail, he wrote

on the edges of newspapers. He even wrote on toilet paper. In this letter, Martin said that people should obey just laws, but they should disobey unjust laws. Even so, he said, they should always behave peacefully. And people should be ready to accept punishment for disobeying the laws.

Martin willingly served his time in jail. After eight days, he was released. Martin could see the light of day again.

Now one of Martin's advisers had a new plan. He wanted to organize a "children's march." At first, Martin was against this plan. Wasn't it too dangerous? But Martin's advisers did not think that the police would throw children in jail.

Thousands of Birmingham children—from six-year-olds to teenagers—were trained in peaceful protest. They joined together in marches. And, yes—some children were put in jail.

On May 2, a huge demonstration was planned. Thousands of young people wanted to take part. At one black school, the principal locked up the gates to keep the students inside. But they climbed over the gates. This march was too important to miss. They were marching for freedom.

Bull Connor and his men came to the march, too. They brought clubs to beat the protesters. Police dogs ripped at the marchers' clothes. The police knocked down people with blasts of water from giant fire hoses. Then the home of Martin's

brother was fire bombed. Other bombs were set around the city.

But reporters were there, too. And cameramen. They wrote stories. They filmed what was happening. By the 1960s, most American homes had a television. Through television, people became more connected to the outside world. It is one thing to read about an attack in a newspaper. It is quite different to see it happening on TV. Martin understood the power of television. He was glad that this struggle was being brought into people's living rooms on a daily basis. Americans were outraged!

Many white business leaders in Birmingham were fed up. But what upset many the most was not the violence, but all the lost business. They held a meeting and decided to give in on some of the marchers' demands. These were some of the promises:

• Lunch counters, restrooms, fitting rooms, and drinking fountains would be desegregated.

• Blacks would be able to get better jobs.

• The protesters in jail would be released.

• A committee of black people and white people would be formed to help ease tensions between the races.

At last, the Jim Crow laws in Birmingham were gone. Martin had won a great victory!

Chapter 8
I Have a Dream

Birmingham proved to black people all around the country what protesting could do. From North Carolina to Tennessee to Oklahoma, black Americans marched and held sit-ins. They held protests in front of government buildings. Gradually, thousands of lunch counters, hotels, schools, and parks became integrated.

Then, on June 11, 1963, President Kennedy asked Congress to pass a civil rights bill. Kennedy said, "I am . . . asking the Congress to enact legislation giving all Americans the right to be served in facilities which are open to the public— hotels, restaurants and

theaters, retail stores and similar establishments. This seems to me to be an elementary right."

On August 28, 1963, Martin and other black leaders led a march to Washington, D.C. They wanted to show Congress how many people supported the civil rights bill. More than two hundred and fifty thousand Americans came from all over the United States. Many rode in cars and buses. Others flew in airplanes. Some walked. Some roller-skated.

Most of the marchers were black. But there were also thousands of white people. They, too, felt that the laws of segregation were unjust. The people marched toward the Lincoln Memorial, singing along the way.

Many leaders spoke that day, but Martin was unforgettable. Martin had written a speech. But he did not read it. Facing the crowd, he remembered a speech he'd given a few months before.

In that speech, he had used the phrase "I have a dream" over and over to express his hopes for the future. Martin wanted to use those same words again. So he put down his script and spoke. His dream was "that one day on the red hills of Georgia the sons of former slaves and the sons of former slave owners will be able to sit down together at the table of brotherhood. . . ." He had a dream that one day people would judge his four young children for who they were and not by the color of their skin.

Martin's speech ended on a powerful note of hope. He believed that, when that day came, everyone could join hands and sing the words to an old slave song: "Free at last, free at last. Thank God Almighty, we are free at last."

The march and Martin Luther King, Jr.'s speech were carried on television stations. It was the first time millions of Americans heard Martin speak. His words inspired the crowd. His words inspired the nation. His words inspired the entire world. Because of this speech, Martin Luther King, Jr., became  the voice of the civil rights movement.

THE GETTYSBURG ADDRESS

ALMOST EXACTLY ONE HUNDRED YEARS BEFORE
PRESIDENT KENNEDY'S SPEECH TO CONGRESS ABOUT
THE CIVIL RIGHTS
BILL, PRESIDENT
ABRAHAM LINCOLN
DELIVERED THE

GETTYSBURG ADDRESS. IT, TOO, WAS ABOUT
CIVIL RIGHTS. IT IS STILL ONE OF THE MOST
FAMOUS SPEECHES IN AMERICAN HISTORY.

ON NOVEMBER 19, 1863, PRESIDENT LINCOLN
SPOKE ABOUT FREEDOM AND DEMOCRACY. IT
WAS DURING THE CIVIL WAR AND HE GAVE THE
SPEECH IN GETTYSBURG, PENNSYLVANIA, WHERE
A GREAT BATTLE HAD BEEN WON BY THE NORTH.

HE SAID THAT "FOURSCORE AND SEVEN
YEARS AGO," OR EIGHTY-SEVEN
YEARS EARLIER, THE NATION WAS
FORMED WITH THE IDEA THAT "ALL
MEN ARE CREATED EQUAL." HE
WANTED A "GOVERNMENT OF
THE PEOPLE, BY THE PEOPLE,
FOR THE PEOPLE."

YET, ONE HUNDRED YEARS
AFTER THE GETTYSBURG
ADDRESS, LINCOLN'S DREAMS
OF EQUALITY WERE STILL NOT
FULLY REALIZED.

But just two weeks later, on September 15, 1963, disaster struck. A blast rocked the early morning silence in Birmingham, Alabama. A bomb went off in the Sixteenth Street Baptist Church. Four black girls lay dead. They were Denise McNair, age eleven; Carole Robertson, age fourteen; Cynthia Wesley, age fourteen; and Addie Mae Collins, age fourteen. The Ku Klux Klan (KKK), a white supremacist terrorist group, committed these murders. (White supremacists believe that white people are superior to non-white people.)

People all around the country were shocked. Martin was filled with grief and bitterness. He contacted President Kennedy to say that he was going to Birmingham to make sure that there was no violent reaction by blacks to the bombing.

President Kennedy sent twenty-five FBI agents and bomb experts to investigate.

Then, on November 22, 1963, disaster struck again. President John F. Kennedy was shot dead in Dallas, Texas. He was the fourth U.S. president to be killed while in office.

The vice president, Lyndon B. Johnson, became president. Five days after President Kennedy's death, President Johnson spoke to Congress. He asked them to pass the civil rights bill that Kennedy had wanted. This was the best way to honor President Kennedy's memory. Congress agreed. On July 2, 1964—almost one hundred years after the country saw the end of slavery— President Johnson signed the Civil Rights Act. And standing next to President Johnson when he signed the bill was Martin Luther King, Jr.

MAJOR FEATURES OF THE
CIVIL RIGHTS ACT OF 1964

• ANYONE COULD REGISTER TO VOTE. LITERACY TESTS (TO SEE IF VOTERS, BOTH BLACK AND WHITE, COULD READ AND WRITE) COULD STILL BE GIVEN.

• DISCRIMINATION IN HOTELS, MOTELS, RESTAURANTS, AND OTHER PUBLIC PLACES WAS OUTLAWED.

• THE ATTORNEY GENERAL COULD TAKE SEGREGATED SCHOOLS TO COURT.

• MONEY WOULD BE TAKEN AWAY FROM ANY STATE PROGRAMS THAT PRACTICED DISCRIMINATION.

• COMPANIES WITH MORE THAN FIFTEEN EMPLOYEES COULD NOT DISCRIMINATE AMONG THE WORKERS.

Chapter 9
The Peace Prize

Martin showed people all over the world the power of words, not fists. In 1964, Martin was awarded the Nobel Peace Prize. This award is given almost every year to the person or group who has done something important in the cause of world peace.

Martin was very grateful for this award. But he knew it wasn't his alone—it belonged to the thousands of brave people who had taken part in the nonviolent fight for equal rights. Martin gave away all the prize money—fifty-four thousand dollars—to civil rights groups.

NOBEL PEACE PRIZE

ALFRED B. NOBEL WAS A SWEDISH CHEMIST AND ENGINEER WHO INVENTED DYNAMITE. WHEN NOBEL DIED IN 1896, HE LEFT NINE MILLION DOLLARS IN HIS WILL TO ESTABLISH THE NOBEL PRIZE. THE PRIZES ARE AWARDED ALMOST EVERY YEAR IN SIX CATEGORIES: PEACE, LITERATURE, PHYSICS, CHEMISTRY, PHYSIOLOGY OR MEDICINE, AND ECONOMICS. MANY DIFFERENT PEOPLE—FROM TEACHERS TO JUDGES TO POLITICIANS—CAN BE NOMINATED FOR AN AWARD. IN SOME YEARS, AS MANY AS TWO HUNDRED NOMINATIONS ARE RECEIVED.

THE NOBEL PEACE PRIZE HAS BEEN AWARDED TO MANY PEOPLE AND ORGANIZATIONS SINCE 1901. SOME PAST WINNERS INCLUDE:

- PRESIDENT BARACK OBAMA—2009
- PRESIDENT JIMMY CARTER—2002
- NELSON MANDELA—1993
- ELIE WIESEL—1986
- MOTHER TERESA—1979

Martin Luther King, Jr., had won the Nobel Peace Prize, but he knew he had not reached his goal: equality for all people. He thought about the defeat in Albany and the success in Birmingham. Surely there were other cities where Martin could help end segregation.

Martin's eyes turned toward Selma, Alabama. Although half of Selma's residents were black, only 1 percent was registered to vote. The voting office was only open a few days a month, which made it difficult for people to register. In addition, the literacy test was so hard, Martin said that even the chief justice of the Supreme Court might not know some answers.

For weeks Martin led groups to the courthouse to register to vote. But it was not legal to hold marches in Selma. So the groups were arrested. Thousands of black people were sent to jail just because they wanted the right to vote.

On February 1, 1965, Martin Luther King, Jr.,

was arrested during one of the marches. While Martin was in jail, a group called the Student Nonviolent Coordinating Committee invited a man named Malcolm X to Selma to speak.

Malcolm X was a young black leader who disagreed with Martin's peaceful protests. Malcolm X did not believe in fighting with words alone. He thought it was okay to use your fists, and more. Malcolm X also spoke about "black pride"—how blacks should respect themselves, and be proud of their race.

While Martin Luther King, Jr., was in jail, he wrote a letter that was published in *The New York Times*. In the letter, Martin said, "There are more Negroes in jail with me than there are on the voting rolls."

Marches spread to many counties in Alabama. One night, a black marcher, Jimmie Lee Jackson, was shot during the voter registration drive. He was twenty-six years old. Before he died, Jimmie Lee said that a state trooper had gunned him down. The black community in Selma was outraged. But Martin still did not want people to fight back with more violence. He thought Malcolm X was wrong. So Martin organized a march from Selma to Montgomery, the capital of Alabama, to demand voting rights for black people.

At the time, the governor of Alabama was George Wallace. He did not want the march to take place. He put a ban on it. Did this stop Martin? No. On March 7, six hundred and fifty marchers set out for Montgomery. Since this was a Sunday, Martin stayed back at his church in Atlanta to preach. He planned to take a plane to Montgomery later that day to meet up with the marchers.

As usual, the protesters were marching in peace. But soon, state troopers, armed with nightsticks and tear gas, appeared. They attacked the group. Some state troopers on horseback trampled the marchers. About seventy people were injured. The violence was captured by television cameras. People all over the country were so angry about what had happened that they protested in their own cities.

Martin, too, was horrified at the news. He also felt guilty about not being with the marchers. So he planned another march two days later.

On March 9, Martin led a group of fifteen hundred from Selma toward Montgomery. Beforehand, Martin told people to leave the line if they had any doubts about remaining. He had to be sure that they wouldn't fight back even if they were beaten up. As they crossed a bridge, the marchers faced a wall of state troopers. Martin saw that many would be hurt, even killed. Marching was one thing. Getting murdered was another. So he turned the group around.

Then good news arrived. Very good news. President Johnson said the protesters had the right to march. He promised to send in troops to protect the marchers.

Suddenly, people from all over the country wanted to join in. On March 21, the group set out—Protestants, Catholics, Jews, blacks, and whites, all marching together.

To Martin, it was a beautiful sight. People walked through quiet valleys and over steep hills. They walked along the highways, stopping only to rest for a minute or two. Their bodies ached. Their feet were sore. But their hearts were light.

By the time they reached Montgomery, they were twenty-five thousand strong. At the state capitol building, they handed a petition to

Governor George Wallace, demanding voting rights for black Americans.

On August 6, 1965, President Johnson signed the Voting Rights Act. President Johnson said, "Every American citizen must have an equal right to vote. Yet the harsh fact is that in many places in this country, men and women are kept from voting simply because they are Negroes."

Now there would be no more literacy tests. And United States government workers would be in charge of registering voters. The Selma freedom marchers had won!

CIVIL RIGHTS LEADERS
WHO GAVE THEIR LIVES FOR THEIR CAUSE

MEDGAR EVERS WAS FROM MISSISSIPPI. GROWING UP, HE ALWAYS QUESTIONED THE JIM CROW LAWS. BY THE TIME HE WAS IN COLLEGE, HE STARTED LOCAL CHAPTERS OF THE NAACP. AND, AFTER BEING TURNED DOWN BY THE UNIVERSITY OF MISSISSIPPI LAW

Medgar Evers

SCHOOL, HE FOUGHT FOR THE DESEGREGATION OF THE SCHOOL. ON JUNE 12, 1963, EVERS WAS KILLED. HE WAS THIRTY-SEVEN YEARS OLD.

A WHITE MAN NAMED BYRON DE LA BECKWITH WAS ACCUSED OF THE MURDER. HE STOOD TRIAL TWICE IN THE 1960S. BUT THE ALL-WHITE JURIES IN BOTH CASES COULD NOT DECIDE IF HE WAS GUILTY OR INNOCENT.

FINALLY, IN A THIRD TRIAL, IN 1994—THIRTY-ONE YEARS AFTER EVERS'S DEATH—BECKWITH WAS FOUND GUILTY. HE WAS SENTENCED TO LIFE IN PRISON.

ANDREW GOODMAN WAS FROM NEW YORK CITY. IN 1964, GOODMAN, AND **MICKEY SCHWERNER**, WHO WAS FROM PHILADELPHIA, WENT TO MISSISSIPPI TO

REGISTER BLACKS TO VOTE. (BOTH
ANDREW GOODMAN AND MICKEY
SCHWERNER WERE WHITE.) ON THE
NIGHT OF JUNE 20, 1964, THE TWO
REACHED MERIDIAN, MISSISSIPPI.
THERE, A BLACK MAN NAMED **JAMES**

Mickey Schwerner

CHANEY JOINED THE GROUP. THE

James Chaney

THREE CIVIL RIGHTS WORKERS WERE
ARRESTED FOR SPEEDING AND TOLD
TO LEAVE TOWN. BUT MEMBERS OF
THE KKK TRACKED THEM DOWN AND
KILLED THEM. THEY WERE ALL
YOUNG MEN WHEN THEY DIED—
GOODMAN WAS TWENTY-ONE,
SCHWERNER WAS TWENTY-FIVE, AND CHANEY
WAS TWENTY-ONE.

IN 1967, NINETEEN WHITE MEN WERE ARRESTED FOR
THE DEATHS OF THE THREE CIVIL RIGHTS WORKERS.
SEVEN OF THE MEN WERE FOUND GUILTY. TWO MEN,
E. G. BARNETT, WHO WAS RUNNING FOR SHERIFF OF
MERIDIAN, AND EDGAR RAY KILLEN, A LOCAL MINISTER,
WERE SET FREE BECAUSE THE JURY COULD NOT
REACH A DECISION. IT WASN'T UNTIL ALMOST FORTY
YEARS LATER, IN 2005, THAT KILLEN WAS ALSO
FOUND GUILTY OF THE MURDERS.

Chapter 10
Fighting Poverty

Even with the right to vote, even with the right to sit anywhere on a bus or eat in any restaurant, black people were struggling. Too many did not have jobs. And those with jobs weren't making enough to live decently. They lived in homes with no heat and leaky pipes. Many people were sick and did not have money to see a doctor.

Black people were angry. They were frustrated. Some were tired of listening to Martin. Change wasn't coming fast enough. People who had followed Malcolm X, who was killed in 1965, were forming groups to carry on his message of fighting back with violence. Groups such as the Black Panther Party emerged. These groups talked about black pride.

In August 1965, a riot broke out in a Los Angeles neighborhood called Watts. Angry mobs of black people ran through the streets. They threw rocks and bottles. They shattered store windows. They stole. They set fires. Many people were killed and injured. The rioting went on for six days. Finally, the U.S. Army was called in to stop the violence.

WATTS RIOTS

ON AUGUST 11, 1965, A BLACK MAN NAMED
MARQUETTE FRYE WAS PULLED OVER WHILE
DRIVING ON A CALIFORNIA HIGHWAY. A POLICE
OFFICER LATER SAID HE WAS DRIVING
DANGEROUSLY.

AS THE POLICE
QUESTIONED FRYE AND
HIS BROTHER, A GROUP
OF PEOPLE GATHERED.
THEY WERE ANGRY.
SOME PEOPLE BEGAN
TO SHOUT AT THE
OFFICERS. THEY
SAID THE FRYE
BROTHERS WERE
ONLY PULLED
OVER BECAUSE
THEY WERE BLACK.
SOME PEOPLE
THREW ROCKS.
WHEN FRYE
AND HIS BROTHER

WERE ARRESTED, THE CROWD GREW ANGRIER AND
BEGAN RIOTING. THE RIOT LASTED FOR SIX DAYS.
IN WATTS, PEOPLE FELT DESPERATE AND
HOPELESS. THEY FELT LIKE VICTIMS.

Martin understood people's frustration. But he said, "When people are voiceless, they will have temper tantrums like a little child who has not been paid attention to. And riots are massive temper tantrums from a neglected and voiceless people."

In response, one of the angry rioters said to Martin, "We know that a riot is not the answer, but we've been down here suffering for a long time and nobody cared. Now at least they know we're here. A riot may not be *the* way, but it is *a* way."

The root of the problem was poverty. People were sick of being poor. So Martin turned his attention to employment—getting better jobs. On July 26, 1965, he led a march to Chicago City Hall.

Chicago was the second largest city in the United States. More than one million blacks lived there. Some people called Chicago "the Birmingham of the North." Most blacks living in

Chicago were poor. They had low-paying jobs or no jobs at all. People lived in old, rundown houses. Although there were laws against segregation, white-owned buildings would not rent apartments to blacks.

In 1966, the Kings moved to Chicago. They were used to living in comfortable houses. But Martin thought it was important for his family to know the way too many blacks in the United States lived. They paid ninety dollars a month for a

rundown, four-room apartment. A much nicer, five-room apartment in a white neighborhood cost only eighty dollars a month!

After a while, Martin's children began to have temper tantrums. At first, Martin couldn't understand why. But then he realized that they were misbehaving because they had nowhere to play. There was no park nearby where they could run around. Martin began to understand what being dirt-poor felt like.

Martin led many marches in Chicago that summer. Although Martin's marchers were not violent, they were met by violence. Bricks and bottles were thrown at them. People yelled at them. Still, none of the protestors fought back.

Martin Luther King, Jr., marched to Chicago City Hall. He posted a list of demands on the door for Mayor Richard J. Daley to read. The demands included an end to police violence and an end to job and housing discrimination.

There was no answer from Mayor Daley. So the marches continued.

Jesse Jackson, a young member of the SCLC, planned a march through a neighborhood called Cicero. Seventy thousand white people

Jesse Jackson

lived there. Mayor Daley and the police knew that a march through Cicero would end in violence. So, finally, the mayor told Martin Luther King, Jr., to call off the march. The demands would be met.

So, in good faith, Martin and the leaders of the SCLC agreed. As for Mayor Daley, he went back on his promise. Nothing changed in Chicago. Where would Martin Luther King, Jr., go from here?

Mayor Daley

Chapter 11
March On

If he couldn't get a city government to cooperate, Martin decided to go higher up. Martin and the Southern Christian Leadership Conference planned another march to Washington, D.C., for the spring of 1968. The purpose was to get Congress to pass laws that would help poor people get better jobs.

Before the big march, Martin Luther King, Jr., went to Memphis, Tennessee. Garbage workers were on strike. Martin wanted to help them get a pay raise.

On March 28, 1968, Martin and the peaceful protestors set out on the streets of Memphis. Once again, the result was violence. But it was caused by some of the marchers. Some teenagers broke into local stores and stole things. A riot began. This went against everything that Martin stood for. Martin returned home to Atlanta and did not come back to Memphis until April 3. Many people were threatening to hurt Martin. But Martin was not afraid. He still hoped to help the striking garbage workers.

Martin met with some of the other city and civil rights leaders the next day. Later that evening, Martin stepped out onto the balcony of his room at the Lorraine Motel. It was chilly outside, but Martin was enjoying the fresh air. Suddenly, a gunshot rang out. Martin fell to the floor.

Martin Luther King, Jr., was dead. The civil rights movement had lost its strongest voice.

JAMES EARL RAY

ON JUNE 8, 1968, A WHITE MAN NAMED JAMES EARL RAY WAS ARRESTED FOR KILLING MARTIN LUTHER KING, JR. JAMES EARL RAY WAS BORN IN ALTON, ILLINOIS, ON MARCH 10, 1928. RAY WAS A SMALL-TIME CRIMINAL. HE ROBBED GAS STATIONS AND STORES. HE WAS IN PRISON THREE TIMES— ONCE IN ILLINOIS AND TWICE IN MISSOURI.

James Earl Ray

AFTER RAY WAS ARRESTED, HE CONFESSED. HE WAS SENTENCED TO NINETY-NINE YEARS IN PRISON. HOWEVER, RAY LATER CLAIMED HE WAS INNOCENT BUT COULD NEVER PROVE IT. IN 1998, RAY DIED IN PRISON.

Chapter 12
The Dream Lives On

Martin Luther King, Jr., was one of the greatest civil rights leaders of all time. Today, people around the world still remember all he did in his fight for equality.

After Martin's death, Coretta carried on her husband's fight. She traveled around the world and talked about peace. She fought to end apartheid, which was a system of segregation in South Africa. Coretta fought for civil rights until her death in 2006.

Martin's children carried on their father's message, too. In 1997, Martin Luther King III was elected to head the Southern Christian Leadership Conference. He stayed with the SCLC until 2004. And Martin's youngest daughter, Bernice, is a minister. She travels around the world speaking about civil rights.

Martin's youngest son, Dexter, attended Morehouse College. In 1997, Dexter visited James Earl Ray in prison. After speaking with Ray, Dexter was convinced that this man had not shot his father.

Martin's oldest child, Yolanda, was an actress, author, and peace advocate. Yoki appeared in several films, including a miniseries about her father called *King*. She died on May 16, 2007. She was fifty-one years old.

In 1980, Martin's boyhood home on Auburn Avenue in Atlanta and other buildings nearby were turned into a National Historic Site. Today,

visitors can go to the museum to learn about Martin Luther King, Jr.'s role in the civil rights movement.

And in 1983, President Ronald Reagan signed a bill to create a federal holiday to honor Martin.

It is observed on the third Monday of January each year, near the time of his birthday.

In his very last sermon on April 3, 1968, Martin Luther King, Jr., talked about his own death. He hoped that people would remember him as a man who "tried to give his life serving others." He wanted to be remembered for helping "to feed the hungry" and for loving people. Fifty years later, people remember Martin Luther King, Jr., and honor him for all this and more.

Martin Luther King, Jr.

TIMELINE OF MARTIN LUTHER KING, JR.'S LIFE

1929 — Born in Atlanta, Georgia

1948 — Graduates from Morehouse College

1951 — Graduates from Crozer

1953 — Marries Coretta Scott

1954 — Becomes pastor of the Dexter Avenue Baptist Church in Montgomery, Alabama

1955–1956 — Leads the Montgomery bus boycott

1957 — Speaks at the Prayer Pilgrimage in Washington, D.C., and asks the government to pass a Civil Rights Bill

1960 — Moves with his family to Atlanta, Georgia; arrested at a sit-in at a whites-only lunch counter in Atlanta

1963 — Leads a boycott of white-owned businesses in Birmingham, Alabama; delivers his "I Have a Dream" speech at a rally in Washington, D.C.

1964 — Awarded the Nobel Peace Prize

1965 — Leads a peaceful march from Selma to Montgomery, Alabama, demanding voting rights for black Americans

1968 — Assassinated in Memphis, Tennessee

TIMELINE OF
THE WORLD

Anne Frank, who died in the Holocaust, is born; — **1929**
Babe Ruth hits his five hundredth home run

Franklin D. Roosevelt is elected president of — **1932**
the United States

Adolf Hitler declares himself the leader of Germany; — **1934**
Wheaties begins putting pictures of athletes on cereal boxes

The Japanese bomb Pearl Harbor in Hawaii, — **1941**
and the United States enters WWII

The first Archie comic book is published — **1942**

World War II ends — **1945**

Jackie Robinson joins the Brooklyn Dodgers, — **1947**
the first African American in modern times to play
on a major league baseball team

The first Mr. Potato Head toy is sold — **1952**

Rosa Parks refuses to give up her seat on a bus in — **1955**
Montgomery, Alabama

Elvis Presley records his song "Heartbreak Hotel" — **1956**

John F. Kennedy is elected president — **1960**

The Berlin Wall is built, dividing the city into democratic — **1961**
West Berlin and communist East Berlin

President John F. Kennedy is assassinated — **1963**

Charlie and the Chocolate Factory by Roald Dahl is published — **1964**

President Johnson sends more troops to Vietnam — **1965**

BIBLIOGRAPHY

Adler, David A. **Dr. Martin Luther King, Jr.** Holiday House, New York, 2003.

Brown, Jonatha A. **People We Should Know: Martin Luther King Jr.** Weekly Reader Early Learning Library, Wisconsin, 2005.

Carson, Clayborne, editor. **The Autobiography of Martin Luther King, Jr.** Warner Books, New York, 1998.

de Kay, James T. **Meet Martin Luther King, Jr.** Random House, New York, 1969.

Myers, Walter Dean. **I've Seen the Promised Land: The Life of Dr. Martin Luther King, Jr.** HarperCollins, New York, 2004.

Peck, Ira. **The Life and Words of Martin Luther King Jr.** Scholastic, Inc., New York, 1991.

Rappaport, Doreen. **Martin's Big Words: The Life of Dr. Martin Luther King, Jr.** Jump at the Sun / Hyperion, New York, 2001.

YOUR HEADQUARTERS FOR HISTORY

Activities, Mad Libs, and sidesplitting jokes!
Discover the Who HQ books beyond the biographies

Who? What? Where?

Learn more at whohq.com!